A HOW ANIMALS LIVE Book

A Time for

SLEEPING

A Time for

SLEEPING

Ron Hirschi

PHOTOGRAPHS BY *Thomas D. Mangelsen*

COBBLEHILL BOOKS/Dutton
New York

For Emma.
—R.H.

For Paul.
—T.M.

Library of Congress Cataloging-in-Publication Data
Hirschi, Ron.
    A time for sleeping / Ron Hirschi ; photographs by Thomas D.
Mangelsen.
        p.   cm. —(A How animals live book)
    Summary: Examines the ways different animals sleep, when they
sleep, and where.
    ISBN 0-525-65128-4
    1. Sleep behavior in animals—Juvenile literature.   [1. Animals—
Sleep behavior.]   I. Mangelsen, Thomas D., ill.   II. Title.
III. Series.
QL755.3.H57   1993
591.51—dc20   92-21408   CIP   AC

Published in the United States by Cobblehill Books,
an affiliate of Dutton Children's Books, a division of
Penguin Books USA Inc., 375 Hudson Street, New York, New York 10014
Designed by Charlotte Staub
Printed in Hong Kong
First edition 10 9 8 7 6 5 4 3 2 1

Polar bear

Even in the cold, cold snow,
even when the icy winds still blow,
sleepy eyes will close.

Then it is time
to curl up tight, crawl
into a soft safe place,
or cuddle close to
someone warm.

Polar bear and cub

Great horned owls

Time for sleep
comes high up in a nest
where wind whispers
through dancing leaves,

on smooth stones
warmed by the noonday
sun,

Chuckwalla

Sea lions

and on top of
wave-washed rocks
surrounded by the
deep blue sea.

Harbor seal

Sea otter wrapped in kelp sleeping

The sparkling waves
rock baby otters to sleep,
safe in tangles of kelp
or wrapped in mother's
arms.

Mule deer fawn

Safe from harm,
baby deer begin their
naps in the
shade.

Mountain sheep
rest with fathers,
uncles, and grand-
fathers near.
Mothers, aunts,
and grandmothers
sleep in separate
groups.

Dall sheep

Coyote

Coyotes yawn.

Rabbits rest
or pop into their
nest. They sit still as
stars and quiet as the
faraway moon.

Eastern cottontail

Arctic fox

Do foxes dream
of rabbits in
their sleep?
Do they twitch fox paws
and fox toes while dreaming
of running, chasing, and
leaping as high as
foxes can leap?

Northern saw-whet owl

Tired from flying
and tired from searching

Black-capped chickadee

all day
for some food,
sleepy birds rest

Cassin's finch

Flycatcher

in the branches of

Purple finch

their favorite trees.

Tired from swimming, tired from winter cold in high mountain lakes, sleepy swans tuck their heads under soft wings for a nap.

Trumpeter swans

Lions

Tired from playing
and tired from sneaking
up on one another,
sleepy kittens close
their eyes too.

Some animals sleep by day.
Some sleep by moonlight.

Northern pygmy owl

All sleep with eyes closed—
closed just so tight.

Afterword

We usually don't think too much about sleeping. Night comes, we yawn a couple of times, our eyes grow tired, then we go to bed and sleep until morning. But imagine sleeping all winter like a hibernating bear. Or imagine sleeping all day long, then prowling the forest by night in search of food like a bobcat, cougar, or a woodland owl.

We usually cover ourselves when we sleep. And, we generally wear separate clothing just for the nighttime. But other animals must make do with their own feathers, fur, or scales when they sleep. They sleep on the ground, in burrows, or in nests. Rarely, they have the comforts of anything nearly as soft as our beds. They do try to find safe places to sleep, especially for young ones or for long resting periods such as hibernation.

Time for sleeping is a critical time for all animals and the resting habitat, or place needed for sleep, is a separate and vital need that is unique for each species. Try to discover the sleeping places of animals near your home, protecting these special places as you would your own bedroom. Animals need their sleep. They need their sleeping places. It is up to each of us to keep these places safe and secure.